False Images, Deadly Promises

SMOKING AND THE MEDIA

Tobacco: The Deadly Drug

False Images, Deadly Promises

SMOKING AND THE MEDIA

by
Ann Malaspina

False Images, Deadly Promises: Smoking and the Media

MASON CREST PUBLISHERS INC.
370 Reed Road
Broomall, Pennsylvania 19008
(866)MCP-BOOK (toll free)
www.masoncrest.com

First Printing

9 8 7 6 5 4 3 2 1

ISBN 978-1-4222-0233-3
ISBN 978-1-4222-0230-2 (series)

Library of Congress Cataloging-in-Publication Data
Malaspina, Ann, 1957–
  False images, deadly promises : smoking and the media / Ann
Malaspina.
    p. cm. — (Tobacco: the deadly drug)
  Includes bibliographical references and index.
  ISBN 978-1-4222-0233-3   ISBN 978-1-4222-1329-2
  1. Smoking—United States. 2. Tobacco industry--United States.
3. Teenagers—Tobacco use—United States. 4. Mass media and
teenagers—United States. 5. Marketing—United States. 6. Mass
media. I. Title.
  HV5760.M37 2009
  659.19′679730973—dc22
                          2008019474
Design by MK Bassett-Harvey.
Produced by Harding House Publishing Service, Inc.
www.hardinghousepages.com
Cover design by Peter Culotta.
Printed in The United States of America.

Contents

Introduction

Tobacco has been around for centuries. In fact, it played a major role in the early history of the United States. Tobacco use has fallen into and out of popularity, sometimes based on gender roles or class, or more recently, because of its effects on health. The books in the Mason Crest series TOBACCO: THE DEADLY DRUG, provide readers with a look at many aspects of tobacco use. Most important, the series takes a serious look at why smoking is such a hard habit to break, even with all of the available information about its harmful effects.

The primary ingredient in tobacco products that keeps people coming back for another cigarette is nicotine. Nicotine is a naturally occurring chemical in the tobacco plant. As plants evolved over millions of years, they developed the ability to produce chemical defenses against being eaten by animals. Nicotine is the tobacco plant's chemical defense weapon. Just as too much nicotine can make a person feel dizzy and nauseated, so the same thing happens to animals that might otherwise eat unlimited quantities of the tobacco plant.

Nicotine, in small doses, produces mildly pleasurable (rewarding) experiences, leading many people to dose themselves repeatedly throughout the day. People carefully dose themselves with nicotine to maximize the rewarding experience. These periodic hits of tobacco also help people avoid unpleasant (toxic) effects, such as dizziness, nausea, trembling, and sweating, which can occur when someone takes in an excessive amount of nicotine. These unpleasant effects are sometimes seen when a person smokes for the first time.

Although nicotine is the rewarding component of cigarettes, it is not the cause of many diseases that trouble smokers, such as lung cancer, heart attacks, and strokes. Many of the thousands of other chemicals in the cigarette are responsible for the increased risk for these diseases among smokers. In some cases, medical research has identified cancer-causing chemicals in the burning cigarette. More research is needed, because our understanding of exactly how cigarette smoking causes many forms of cancer, lung diseases (emphysema, bronchitis), heart attacks, and strokes is limited, as is our knowledge on the effects of secondhand smoke.

The problem with smoking also involves addiction. But what is addiction? Addiction refers to a pattern of behavior, lasting months to years, in which a person engages in the intense, daily use of a pleasure-producing (rewarding) activity, such as smoking. This type of use has medically and personally negative effects for the person. As an example of negative medical consequences, consider that heavy smoking (nicotine addiction) leads to heart attacks and lung cancer. As an example of negative personal consequences, consider that heavy smoking may cause a loss of friendship, because the friend can't tolerate the smoke and/or the odor.

Nicotine addiction includes tolerance and withdrawal. New smokers typically start with fewer than five cigarettes per day. Gradually, as the body becomes adapted to the presence of nicotine, greater amounts are required to obtain the same rewarding effects, and the person eventually smokes fifteen to twenty or more cigarettes per day. This is tolerance, meaning that more drug is needed to achieve the same rewarding effects. The brain becomes "wired" differently after long-term exposure to nicotine, allowing the brain to tolerate levels of nicotine that would otherwise be toxic and cause nausea, vomiting, dizziness and anxiety.

When a heavy smoker abruptly stops smoking, irritability, headache, sleeplessness, anxiety, and difficulty concentrating all develop within half a day and trouble the smoker for one to two weeks. These withdrawal effects are generally the opposite of those produced by the drug. They are another external sign that the brain has become wired differently because of long-term exposure to nicotine. The withdrawal effects described above are accompanied by craving. For the nicotine addict, craving is a state of mind in which having a cigarette seems the most important thing in life at the moment. For the nicotine addict, craving is a powerful urge to smoke.

Nicotine addiction, then, can be understood as heavy, daily use over months to years (with tolerance and withdrawal), despite negative consequences. Now that we have definitions of *nicotine* and *addiction*, why read the books in this series? The answer is simple: tobacco is available everywhere to persons of all ages. The books in the series TOBACCO: THE DEADLY DRUG are about understanding the beginnings, natural history, and consequences of nicotine addiction. If a teenager smokes at least one cigarette daily for a month, that person has an 80 percent chance of becoming a lifetime, nicotine-addicted, daily smoker, with all the negative consequences.

But the series is not limited to those topics. What are the characteristic beginnings of nicotine addiction? Nicotine addiction typically begins between the ages of twelve and twenty, when most young people decide to try a first cigarette. Because cigarettes are available everywhere in our society, with little restriction on purchase, nearly everyone is faced with the decision to take a puff from that first cigarette. Whether this first puff leads to a lifetime of nicotine addiction depends on several factors. Perhaps the most important factor is DNA (genetics), as twin studies tell us that most of the risk for nicotine addiction is genetic, but there is a large role for nongenetic factors (environment), such as the smoking habits of friends. Research is needed to identify the specific genetic and environmental factors that shape a person's decision to continue to smoke after that first cigarette. Books in the series also address how peer pressure and biology affect one's likelihood of smoking and possibly becoming addicted.

It is difficult to underestimate the power of nicotine addiction. It causes smokers to continue to smoke despite life-threatening events. When heavy smokers have a heart attack, a life-threatening event often directly related to smoking, they spend a week or more in the hospital where they cannot smoke. So they are discharged after enforced abstinence. Even though they realize that smoking contributed strongly to the heart attack, half of them return to their former smoking habits within three weeks of leaving the hospital. This decision to return to smoking increases the risk of a second heart attack. Nicotine addiction can influence powerfully the choices we make, often prompting us to make choices that put us at risk.

TOBACCO: THE DEADLY DRUG doesn't stop with the whys and the hows of smoking and addiction. The series includes books that provide readers with tools they can use to not take that first cigarette, how they can stand up to negative peer pressure, and know when they are being unfairly influenced by the media. And if they do become smokers, books in the series provide information about how they can stop.

If nicotine addiction can be a powerful negative effect, then giving people information that might help them decide to avoid—or stop—smoking makes sense. That is what TOBACCO: THE DEADLY DRUG is all about.

— *Wade Berrettini MD, PhD*

CHAPTER

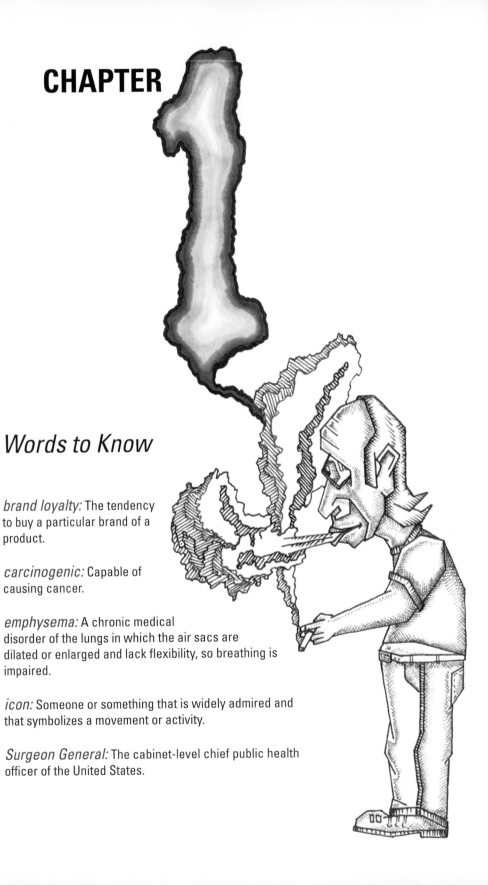

Words to Know

brand loyalty: The tendency to buy a particular brand of a product.

carcinogenic: Capable of causing cancer.

emphysema: A chronic medical disorder of the lungs in which the air sacs are dilated or enlarged and lack flexibility, so breathing is impaired.

icon: Someone or something that is widely admired and that symbolizes a movement or activity.

Surgeon General: The cabinet-level chief public health officer of the United States.

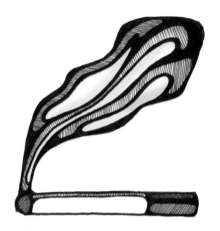

Selling
Smoke

Glamour. Sophistication. Independence. Attitude. Like other marketers of consumer goods—from sports cars to fast food—the tobacco industry invests its products with an irresistible allure. Cigarette advertisements have featured attractive young men and women in a variety of appealing locations: snow-covered mountains, wide-open western prairies, tropical islands. With cigarettes in hand, in their back pockets, or even rolled in the sleeves of their T-shirts (the guys, anyway), the men and women appear popular and successful. For men, cigarettes are shown as symbols of masculinity and athleticism. For women, smoking has been promoted as a way to be

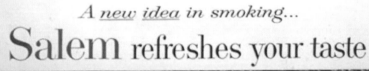

Before legislation was passed that monitored how cigarettes were advertised, many tobacco companies portrayed their products as healthy and "cool."

independent and sophisticated, and to keep attractively slim.

Through the decades, tobacco companies sent the message that every pack contains more than a foil wrapper and twenty cigarettes. "A breath of springtime freshness" in every puff of Salem cigarettes, claimed a 1961 television ad featuring a young woman smoking a cigarette by a waterfall. The cartoon character Joe Camel's quirky personality breathed new life into Camels, an old brand, in the 1980s. In the "B Kool" campaign for Kool cigarettes in the 1990s, the guy with the cigarette always seemed to get the girl's attention. Rather than just buying cigarettes, consumers have been invited to buy a whole new identity.

Provocative Images

For teens, the eye-catching images, along with catchy slogans, have been particularly powerful. According to surveys of high school students by Professor John Pierce of the University of California at San Diego, media images played a major role in the decision to smoke in approximately 34 percent of teenage smokers. "We have shown that before they start smoking, the kids who really liked the advertising start changing their beliefs. They stop believing it's harmful to smoke. And they start believing they can quit when they want to," Pierce observed in 2000 in the online magazine *Salon*. A long-term study of high school students in the 1990s, published by the *American Journal of Public Health* in 2007, confirmed that young adolescents who have a favorite cigarette advertisement or own a cigarette promotional item are more likely than other teens to be smokers by young adulthood.

Tobacco has not been promoted only through advertising; it has also been promoted in less obvious ways. Actors smoking in movies and rock stars lighting up in music videos have become part of contemporary American culture. These media images are not advertisements, but they are just as convincing. They can overwhelm impulses that otherwise might lead teens to choose not to smoke.

Thus, despite the well-known scientific data on the health hazards and addictive dangers of cigarettes, smoking is still seen as cool by many teens. "I like walking around late at night, smoking a cigarette," a teen told the *Pittsburgh Post-Gazette*. "When I'm only walking around, I'm just a little kid. But when I'm walking around and smoking, I'm a little kid with a cigarette."

Part of American Culture

Starting in the 1880s, tobacco companies inserted collecting cards, with photographs of models and baseball players, in cigarette packs to encourage new smokers to buy another pack. In 1913, Camel cigarettes were introduced with a national advertising campaign that began with the promising slogan "The Camels are coming." From billboards to radio jingles, magazine spreads to newspaper ads, cigarette promotions soon became part of the American culture.

Tobacco Cure-All

Native Americans believed tobacco could aid in healing or curing asthma, bad breath, bruises, colic, constipation, convulsions, coughs, cuts, diarrhea, fatigue, fever, gout, headaches, hunger, kidney stones, malaria, miscarriages, pain, paralysis, seizures, sleeplessness, sore muscles, snakebites, sore throat, scorpion stings, stomachaches, toothaches, and even warts.

By the 1950s, Lucy and Ricky Ricardo were trading jokes and cigarettes in commercials for the tobacco giant Philip Morris, a sponsor of the immensely popular *I Love Lucy* show. During the 1960s, the Marlboro Man—a rugged cowboy created by Philip Morris

Camel cigarettes used to be sold in packs with pictures of famous baseball players, linking smoking together with athletes in people's minds and making people more likely to buy more packs in order to collect all the cards.

admen—became a familiar sight to American television viewers. He rode his horse, roped cattle, and smoked his way through the West—Marlboro Country—in countless TV commercials. Later the Marlboro Man became a fixture in billboard and magazine advertising.

In 1964, the U.S. *Surgeon General* released a ground-breaking report detailing the health hazards of cigarette smoke. The report helped spark a crackdown on tobacco advertising aimed at young people. Nevertheless, ad dollars spent on cigarette promotions actually increased over the next two decades.

The Marlboro Man was a famous model in Marlboro cigarette ads. Today, however, many former Marlboro Man models are suffering from various kinds of cancer and lung diseases caused by smoking.

Congress banned cigarette ads on television and radio in 1971, but tobacco companies then turned to in-store ads, magazine spreads, giveaways, and concert and professional sports sponsorships, among other promotions. Sports and tobacco already had a history. Some of the most popular tobacco spokespeople were stars in established sports, such as baseball's Joe DiMaggio in the 1930s and golf pro Arnold Palmer in the 1980s. Tobacco companies also discovered they could get advertising mileage by sponsoring stock car racing, women's professional tennis, and other growing sports. In 1986, millions of television viewers around the world tuned in to the World Cup soccer games in Mexico City and saw stadium billboards advertising Camel cigarettes, a product of R. J. Reynolds, one of the event's sponsors. Cigarettes and sports might have seemed an odd pairing once scientists proved the health hazards of smoking, but the ads caught the attention of many young people fascinated by professional athletics.

Glamour and Danger

Tobacco also planted its roots in Hollywood, where smoking became common in films starting in the 1930s. By the 1980s, tobacco companies were even paying film producers to place their brands in visible spots in movies. For example, Philip Morris paid £20,000 (about $44,000) to have Marlboros featured in the 1980 blockbuster *Superman II*. This practice of tobacco product placement was banned when the major tobacco companies signed an agreement in 1998 to limit advertising, especially to young people. But actors in movies popular with young people did not stop smoking. In recent years, young viewers could catch Cameron Diaz smoking in *Charlie's Angels* and Julia Roberts lighting up in *My Best Friend's*

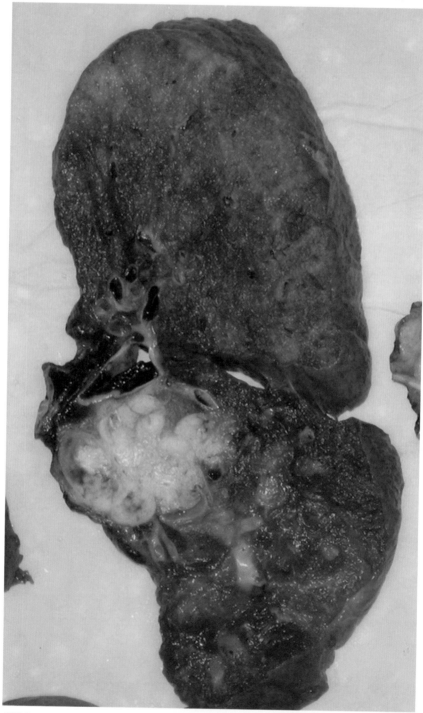

While smoking is often portrayed as glamorous in ads and media, tobacco use can cause lung cancer and other deadly health problems.

Wedding. Even on the small screen, Sarah Jessica Parker bought cartons of Marlboro Lights on *Sex and the City*, and Tony chewed his cigar on *The Sopranos*, two HBO hit shows.

The glamorization of smoking in ads and in the media stands in sharp contrast to the proven dangers of smoking. The tobacco industry is not selling sophistication, wealth, or the chance to be a movie star or top athlete, but a hazardous product. Tobacco use is the leading preventable cause of death in the United States. Smoking-related diseases and illnesses such as lung cancer, *emphysema*, and heart disease claim an estimated 438,000 American lives every year, according to the American Lung Association (ALA), the leading organization fighting lung diseases. Secondhand smoke, or smoke inhaled from other people's cigarettes, is also dangerous. According to the ALA, secondhand smoke is the cause of about 3,400 lung cancer deaths, and about 46,000 deaths from heart disease, in the United States each year.

Food of the Spirits

Tobacco was believed to be the "food of the spirits," and the spirits seemed to have an endless hunger. Since they couldn't grow or eat it themselves, spirits depended on humans to deliver tobacco to them. Therefore, humans consumed tobacco during ritual offerings for the spirits. They believed the spirits would, in turn, bestow good favor and fortune on them.

Cigarette smoke contains some 4,000 chemicals. Dozens are known to be *carcinogenic*, or cancer causing. Toxic gases produced by lit cigarettes include carbon monoxide, hydrogen cyanide, formaldehyde, and ammonia. Cigarette smoke also contains tar, a tacky brown residue. Cigarette filters trap some tar, but much of the substance is inhaled. Over time it accumulates in the

Surgeon General C. Everett Koop recognized that nicotine is as addictive as heroin or cocaine.

smoker's lungs, contributing to diseases such as bronchitis, emphysema, and lung cancer.

Tobacco smoke also contains nicotine. This chemical, which occurs naturally in tobacco leaves, stimulates certain nerve cells and provides pleasurable sensations, making a smoker feel alert or relaxed depending on the dose. Nicotine is highly addictive. In fact, Surgeon General C. Everett Koop declared in 1988 that nicotine is as addictive as heroin or cocaine.

Despite the many risks, teens continue to light up. Each day, approximately 4,000 young people between the ages of twelve and seventeen try their first cigarette. Every day, about 1,140 teens become regular smokers; one-third will eventually die from smoking, the ALA estimates.

"Tomorrow's Cigarette Business"

Nearly 90 percent of smokers start the habit when they are teenagers, according to the U.S. Department of Health and Human Services (HHS). To stay in business and build their brands, tobacco companies need this valuable market. "Beyond the simple fact that they live longer, young smokers [are] desirable for two reasons: the first brand one smokes is likely to be the brand one keeps for life, and the younger someone starts smoking, the less likely they are to be able to quit," writes Allan M. Brandt in *The Cigarette Century: The Rise, Fall, and Deadly Persistence of the Product That Defined America*.

Internal memos from tobacco companies, made public during court cases or by former employees, show that tobacco executives have long focused on ways to build *brand loyalty* among young people. During a 1974 meeting of the board of directors of R. J. Reynolds, the company's vice president for marketing, C. A. Tucker, described young people between the ages of fourteen and twenty-four as "tomorrow's cigarette business" and outlined the ways in which R. J. Reynolds was aiming its marketing campaign toward that age group.

In a document posted online by the Legacy Tobacco Documents Library at the University of California, San Francisco, Tucker stated that it was necessary to "increase the young adult franchise." The way to do it, he said, was through skillful marketing. Tucker went on to say that R. J. Reynolds had increased its efforts to target young adults, in part by advertising in popular magazines like *Sports Illustrated* and *Ms.*

Young people, especially children and young teenagers, are especially susceptible to peer pressure and to appealing advertising by tobacco companies.

Youth Market

Over the years, tobacco marketers developed other ways to reach young people. These included coupons, sponsorship of NASCAR, and promotions at special events attended by youth, such as rock concerts. By the first years of the 21st century, advertising to young people was strictly limited. Yet in-store displays, event sponsorships, and magazine ads continued to promote cigarettes in a manner guaranteed to reach people of all ages. A 2002 study by researchers at the University of Chicago claimed that this wasn't accidental. The three largest tobacco companies, the study's authors said, were still intentionally targeting youth in their ad campaigns, though tobacco companies consistently denied this. "Cigarette companies had to become slightly more subtle about it, but they continue to aim their advertising at people under 18," study coauthor Paul Chung stated.

Vulnerable Teens

Adolescents and young adults are especially vulnerable to marketing and media. As children move into their teen years, their identities are still forming. They are trying to figure out who they are and what kind of adults they are going to become. Teens continually test themselves and the world around them. In general, they are more easily affected by outside influences than are adults.

Yet teens smoke for many reasons, not just because they see ads in convenience stores or see actors smoking in a movie. Along with advertising, easy access to cigarettes and low prices can also influence teen smokers, according to the World Health Organization. Peer pressure and friends who smoke can push a teen to light up for the first time. Some teens are simply curious and want to try something they've heard so much about. Other teens turn to cigarettes as a way to cope with the stress in their lives. Teens with parents who smoke are also more likely to become smokers than teens who grow up in smoke-free homes.

Tobacco companies often sponsored sports events, like this NASCAR race, in an attempt to advertise their product.

Stretching—and even breaking—the rules is part of growing up. Many teens want to test limits and take new risks. Experimentation is common during adolescence, but some experiments have serious consequences. Because nicotine in cigarettes is so addictive, many teenagers who start smoking just to see what it's like find themselves unable to stop. The tobacco industry has long been aware of teens' vulnerability. As R. J. Reynolds executive Claude E. Teague Jr. stated in 1973:

> The adolescent seeks to display his new urge for independence with a symbol, and cigarettes are such a symbol. . . . The fragile, developing self-image of the young person needs all of the support

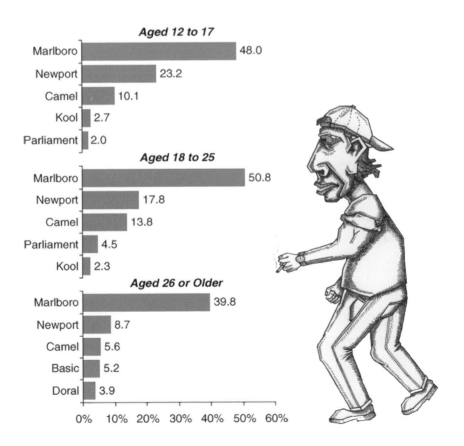

Aged 12 to 17

Marlboro	48.0
Newport	23.2
Camel	10.1
Kool	2.7
Parliament	2.0

Aged 18 to 25

Marlboro	50.8
Newport	17.8
Camel	13.8
Parliament	4.5
Kool	2.3

Aged 26 or Older

Marlboro	39.8
Newport	8.7
Camel	5.6
Basic	5.2
Doral	3.9

0% 10% 20% 30% 40% 50% 60%

Cigarettes are often viewed by teenagers initially as a symbol of independence or rebellion. However, many of these young smokers will end up addicted to nicotine.

and enhancement it can get. Smoking may appear to enhance that self-image in a variety of ways.

He added, in a memo posted online by the Legacy Tobacco Documents Library, "Realistically, if our company is to survive and prosper in the long-term we must get our share of the youth market."

For these same reasons, tobacco critics are trying to protect youth from lighting up their first cigarettes. Educators, teen advocates, medical professionals, and concerned parents strive to make young people aware of smoking's dangers. But industry executives and creative marketing people find ways to cut through the science, often with appealing characters that advocate smoking. Occasionally, one of these characters becomes an advertising *icon*. Joe Camel is perhaps the most notable example.

CHAPTER

Words to Know

cessation: A stop, pause, or interruption in an activity.

point-of-purchase advertising: Advertising (such as in-store displays) that occurs where a product is actually sold.

The Camel Who Played the Sax

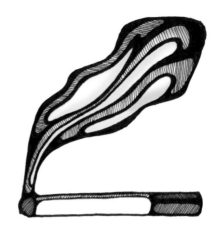

The struggle between the tobacco industry and antismoking advocates wishing to stop cigarette promotions to young people has been long and fierce. One of the biggest battlegrounds was television. The "golden age of tobacco advertising" arrived with the exploding popularity of television, starting in the 1950s. The new medium of communication and entertainment needed sponsors to pay the costs of producing TV shows and to enable the networks to turn a profit. Many early shows relied on tobacco sponsors and aired cigarette ads during commercial breaks. The Winston cigarette brand was a sponsor of *The Flintstones*, the popular cartoon that premiered in 1960 on ABC. Shown during prime time, it was billed as a show for adults and families. As with many tobacco-sponsored shows, the lead characters of *The Flintstones* became spokespeople for the brand. Fred and Barney were featured in Winston ads. In one ad, Fred lit a cigarette for his wife, Wilma. In others, Fred and Barney were seen smoking behind a rock, and Fred said the famous Winston catchphrase, "Winston tastes good like a cigarette should."

But fictional characters weren't the only figures seen smoking on camera in the early days of television broadcasting. Many journalists and talk show hosts also lit up routinely. One of the most famous of these figures was the CBS journalist Edward R. Murrow. Murrow's dramatic radio broadcasts from London during World War II had made him a star, and during the 1950s he hosted an acclaimed television news program, *See It Now*. Ironically, Murrow—who smoked sixty to seventy cigarettes a day—became one of the first journalists to air a report about the health dangers of cigarettes. Lung cancer claimed his life in 1965.

Addictive and Dangerous

Scientific evidence that cigarettes are harmful and addictive began mounting in the 1940s. As early as 1942, the popular magazine *Reader's Digest* published a story, "Cigarette Advertising Fact and Fiction," stating that all cigarette brands were similar and all were hazardous. Tobacco companies fought back, promoting certain brands as being more healthful than others. In 1946, R. J. Reynolds launched its "More Doctors Smoke Camels" campaign and even advertised in medical journals. New brands with lower tar and nicotine levels were introduced. The benefits of filtered cigarettes were also touted. Eventually, however, scientists would determine that the supposedly healthier brands were just as addictive and dangerous.

Internal documents from tobacco companies show that industry leaders were aware of links between heavy

Tobacco companies used to market their products as not only harmless, but actually beneficial to human health. This ad claimed that Camel cigarettes helped to keep your skin clear.

smoking and lung cancer as early as the 1940s and 1950s. But they refused to acknowledge the dangers to the public.

Outside researchers were sounding a warning, though. In 1950, two scientists published a study on smoking in the *Journal of the American Medical Association*. It showed that more than 95 percent of lung-cancer patients were moderately heavy to heavy smokers. The scientists stated: "It appears that the less a person smokes the less are the chances of cancer of the lung developing and the more heavily a person smokes the greater are his chances of becoming affected with this disease."

More than a decade would pass before the government took action, however. On January 11, 1964, the federal government released *Smoking and Health: Report of*

Smoking was recognized to cause cancer as early as 1964, when Luther Terry prepared a document on the effects of smoking for the federal government.

the Advisory Committee to the Surgeon General of the Public Health Service. The 387-page document—prepared under the direction of Surgeon General Luther Terry—gave the first officially recognized proof that smoking causes cancer and other chronic and deadly diseases. Over the next forty years, more than twenty-five additional reports from the office of America's chief health officer would flesh out the many dangers associated with tobacco use.

The release of Terry's groundbreaking report had an immediate impact. Even people who earned a living from tobacco advertising were shocked after reading it. "It was one of the most agonizing weekends I've spent in my life," Wally O'Brien, a copywriter for Liggett & Myers cigarettes in the 1960s and former director general of the International Advertising Association, told *Advertising Age* in 2007. "I didn't know how I could go back to work on Monday morning and still work on that account."

For its part, the tobacco industry responded to public concerns by announcing, in the spring of 1964, the voluntary Cigarette Advertising and Promotion Code. Under the terms set out in the code, which took effect in 1965, tobacco companies promised

Tobacco and the Clergy

After the Spanish conquistadors had subdued a native people, Roman Catholic clergymen arrived to convert the Indians to Christianity. Not surprisingly, priests sometimes adopted Indian habits, including the use of tobacco.

Evidently, some priests took to smoking or snuffing tobacco before church services. Native shamans had used tobacco to communicate with the spirit world, but the Catholic hierarchy took a dim view of priests celebrating Mass in an altered state. In 1583 a decree was issued in Lima, Peru, that banned priests from using tobacco in any way before a church service.

not to advertise or market to youth under the age of twenty-one, or to show sports figures in cigarette ads.

Beginning in 1965, the federal government required all cigarette packages to carry the following warning to consumers: "Caution: Cigarette Smoking May Be Hazardous to Your Health." Over the years, the government would mandate that more strongly worded—and more specific—warnings be placed on all cigarette packages, as well as on all advertisements for cigarettes. In 1984, four alternating messages were established:

- Cigarette Smoke Contains Carbon Monoxide
- Quitting Smoking Now Greatly Reduces Serious Risks to Your Health
- Smoking by Pregnant Women May Result in Fetal Injury, Premature Birth, and Low Birth Weight
- Smoking Causes Lung Cancer, Heart Disease, Emphysema, and May Complicate Pregnancy

But legislation designed to reduce tobacco use wasn't confined to requirements that cigarette makers warn

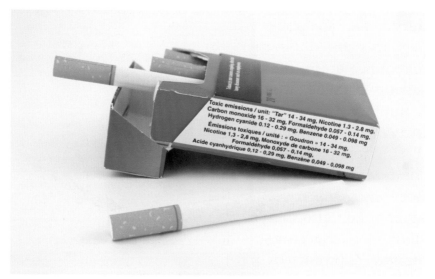

Today, all cigarette packages must feature one of several warnings by the Surgeon Genreal on them in order to be sold.

consumers of the dangers of smoking. The Public Health Cigarette Smoking Act, passed by Congress in 1969 and signed into law the following year by President Richard Nixon, banned all cigarette advertising from radio and television. The ban took effect on January 2, 1971, after the New Year's Day college bowl games. The last cigarette commercial on television was a Virginia Slims ad that aired on the *Tonight Show with Johnny Carson* at 11:59 p.m. on January 1. With the end of television ads, tobacco companies lost a major advertising venue—and television lost an estimated $220 million in ad revenues.

Enter Joe Camel

The tobacco industry still had a product to sell, so it needed to continue reaching consumers. Tobacco companies would have to find new ways to advertise, including some that indirectly or directly affected young people.

By the 1980s, one of the R. J. Reynolds Tobacco Company's oldest brands, Camel, was failing to attract new smokers. Introduced in 1913, Camel was smoked primarily by older men. To revive the brand for Camel's seventy-fifth anniversary, R. J. Reynolds turned to a cartoon mascot, Old Joe Camel. A dromedary with human characteristics, Joe Camel wore sunglasses, played the saxophone, and, of course, smoked Camel cigarettes. He was funny and cool. Joe

Animal Cure-All
Doctor Nicolás Monardes from Seville, Spain, not only suggested using tobacco as a cure for almost any human ailment; he believed the plant would cure animals, too. Monardes said tobacco could cure cattle's wounds, infections, hoof-and-mouth disease, and parasites.

Camel ads began appearing widely, and the company gave away promotional merchandise like free T-shirts and lighters.

The Joe Camel ad campaign was a huge success. As sales of Camel cigarettes rose, critics worried that the cartoon figure appealed to young people. R. J. Reynolds denied that it was targeting youth; the company claimed that its goal was to get male smokers in their twenties to switch to Camel. Still, the cartoon caught young people's attention. According to the American Legacy Foundation, a national tobacco education and anti-smoking organization, Camel's share of the under-eighteen market skyrocketed with the new campaign. The American Medical Association (AMA) released a study in 1991 showing that very young children could identify Joe Camel with more frequency than they could identify

Joe Camel was used as an attempt to make tobacco ads interesting and appealing to a wide range of audiences; however, in 1997, Camel was force to retire this mascot.

Mickey Mouse. Approximately 30 percent of three-year-old children correctly matched Joe Camel with a picture of a cigarette; 91 percent of six-year-olds could correctly identify the advertising icon. The study demonstrated that even very young children were affected by cigarette advertisements. "Given the serious health consequences of smoking, the exposure of children to environmental tobacco advertising may represent an important health risk and should be studied further," the AMA researchers asserted. The AMA requested that the ad campaign be stopped, but R. J. Reynolds did not comply.

Pressure to retire the cigarette mascot continued to mount. In May 1997, the Federal Trade Commission (FTC), the agency that enforces consumer-protection laws, filed a complaint against R. J. Reynolds. The complaint charged that the Joe Camel campaign violated federal law because it appealed to children and adolescents under eighteen and "induced many young people to begin smoking or to continue smoking cigarettes and as a result caused significant injury to their health." Finally, in July 1997, the company formally withdrew Joe Camel from its marketing plans.

But other youth-oriented promotions continued, including the practice of giving away free samples of cigarettes at rock concerts and other gatherings that attracted large numbers of young people. Tobacco companies also sponsored sports, art exhibits, and other cultural events. In 1981, for example, Kool cigarettes took over sponsorship of the famous Newport Jazz Festival, renaming it the Kool Jazz Festival. One of the premier summer music events, the festival was attended by thousands of young people each year.

Tobacco companies used many gimmicks to get people to buy their products. Kool, shown here, gave away free CDs.

Master Settlement Agreement

In the 1990s, many states filed lawsuits against tobacco companies. They wanted to be reimbursed for the cost of providing health care to citizens who suffered from smoking-related illnesses. Thousands of patients had turned to public medical assistance programs to help pay doctors' bills for treating lung cancer, emphysema, and other diseases linked to cigarette smoking. The cost was passed on to the states, which now wanted to be paid back. In 1998, after years of legal battles, the four major tobacco companies signed the Master Settlement Agreement (MSA) with attorneys general in forty-six states (four other states had already signed their own agreements with those tobacco companies). Forty smaller tobacco companies joined the agreement later.

By the terms of the MSA, the states agreed to abandon their individual lawsuits against the tobacco companies. In return, the tobacco companies promised to pay the states $206 billion over twenty-five years to fund education and health programs. The companies also agreed to change the way they marketed cigarettes—specifically, by ending practices that appealed to youth. The companies were to stop using cartoon characters in ads; restrict sponsorship of events with mostly youth audiences, such as concerts; and ban outdoor advertising, such as billboards and ads on buses and trains. The MSA also prohibited tobacco companies from paying for product placement in movies and television and ended the practice of giving youths free cigarette

Outdoor smoking advertisements, like this one, were banned by the MSA.

samples. Finally, tobacco companies promised to fund a public education project, the American Legacy Foundation, for smoking *cessation* and education programs. This marked the end of an era for tobacco promotions.

In-Store Promotions Attract Teens

In the years that followed the MSA, tobacco companies continued to spend billions of dollars on advertising and promotion, though the amount has fallen slightly every year. Tobacco companies spent $13.11 billion on advertising and promotions in 2005, according to the FTC. Nearly

$10 billion of this sum went toward price discounts to retailers and wholesalers. Several studies have shown that tobacco promotions still reach young people.

Coupons and direct-mail advertising continue to be used by tobacco companies. The companies also place display advertising in stores where people buy cigarettes. This is known as *point-of-purchase advertising*. Placing cigarette packs in prominent spots on the shelves, such as behind the checkout counter, and hanging promotional signs on the outside of gas stations or behind the cash registers at convenience stores are standard point-of-purchase promotions. Another widely used method involves price cuts or "buy-one-get-one-free" promotions. Also, companies sometimes offer a free item with the purchase of cigarettes to sway consumers toward a particular brand.

Most retail stores have tobacco ads on inside walls and windows, according to the Campaign for Tobacco-Free Kids, a national advocacy group. Some 80 percent of stores, the group reports, have indoor tobacco advertising, while 60 percent have exterior advertising; 40 percent of gas stations have outside tobacco ads.

Point-of-purchase advertising has been found to be particularly effective in influencing young people. Seeing cigarette ads in a store increases the chance that a young person will start smoking, according to a study published in 2007 in the *Archives of Pediatrics and Adolescent Medicine*. Also, the study suggests, young people are more likely to go from experimenting to regular smoking if stores advertise price cuts or sales on particular cigarette brands. By contrast, when stores reduce cigarette ads, youth smoking declines significantly, the study found.

If stores offer coupons or price cuts in their advertising, young people are
more likely to become regular smokers.

Tobacco companies have long demonstrated a special interest in attracting youth to their products. They've also developed creative marketing campaigns targeted specifically at young women.

CHAPTER 3

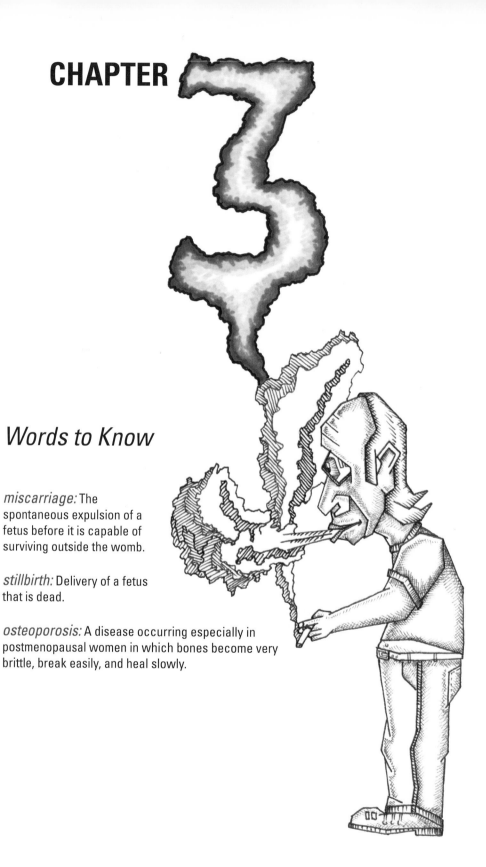

Words to Know

miscarriage: The spontaneous expulsion of a fetus before it is capable of surviving outside the womb.

stillbirth: Delivery of a fetus that is dead.

osteoporosis: A disease occurring especially in postmenopausal women in which bones become very brittle, break easily, and heal slowly.

"You've Come a Long Way, Baby"

Tucked between the lipstick ads and fashion stories in a 2007 issue of *Vogue*, a popular women's magazine, was a glossy ad for a new variety of cigarette. In the center of the ad, bracketed by two stems of blooming flowers, were two slender cigarette boxes. The boxes—black with pink, fuchsia, and mint-green accents—were each emblazoned with the silhouette of a camel. Camel No. 9, whose slogan was "Light & Luscious," was the latest offering from R. J. Reynolds.

The ad created quite a furor. In large part that's because everything about it, critics charged, seemed calculated to appeal to young women. Even the brand, Camel No. 9, echoed the name of a sophisticated perfume, Chanel No. 9. A writer who had lung cancer told the Associated Press: "I wonder if a teenager or a 20-something woman reading the magazines has the willpower to stay away from cigarettes, as she is simultaneously bombarded in neighboring pages with messages about being thin and how to lose fat."

Volunteers from the Campaign for Tobacco-Free Kids, a leading antismoking organization, sent *Vogue* thousands of e-mails and faxes in protest. In response, R. J.

Many tobacco companies, like Camel, tried to portray smoking as glamorous and sexy in an an attempt to attract more women smokers.

Reynolds denied the ads or the brand were aimed at underage smokers.

The company did acknowledge, however, that Camel No. 9s were expected to appeal to women smokers. "We've been forthright from the beginning," an R. J. Reynolds spokesman told the Associated Press. "We launched Camel No. 9 for women who were asking for a product that better reflected their taste preferences and style."

This sort of marketing was nothing new. For decades, tobacco companies had been trying to get women to smoke their cigarettes.

Equal Rights to Vote . . . and Smoke

Until the 1920s, women were discouraged from smoking cigarettes. Women who smoked were widely considered to be of low character and loose morals. Public disapproval of smoking—whether by men or women—emerged during the late nineteenth century, and more than a dozen U.S. states enacted laws banning the sale of cigarettes. But women who lit up elicited special contempt; sometimes they received fairly harsh punishment as well. As author Allan Brandt reports in *The Cigarette Century*, in 1904 a woman in New York was sentenced to thirty days in jail for endangering her children's morals. The woman had smoked in front of the children.

Given this social climate, tobacco companies did not advertise directly to women. Still, cigarette ads prominently featured attractive women.

With the end of World War I in 1918, American women entered a new era. In 1920, the Nineteenth Amendment to the Constitution—which gave American women the right to vote—was ratified. Three years later, women's

rights activists proposed another constitutional amendment. The equal rights amendment (referred to at the
time as the "Lucretia Mott amendment") would elimi-
nate discrimination on the basis of sex.

Many states still tried to limit cigarette sales, use, and
advertising. But smoking was growing more popular
and more acceptable. And if men had a right to smoke,
so did women. In various ways, society moved to
accommodate female smokers. For example, Broadway
theaters opened smoking rooms for women.

By the late 1920s, tobacco companies saw women as
a big new market. George Washington Hill, president of
American Tobacco, said getting women to smoke "will
be like opening a new gold mine in our front yard,"
according to an issue brief published by the National
Research Center on Women and Families. The industry
began reaching out to women with packaging, products,
and slogans. Marlboros were rolled out as a woman's
cigarette. Tobacco ads appealed to women's new sense
of freedom and equality, as well as to their vanity. Hill
launched a campaign for Lucky Strikes aimed directly at
women. "Reach for a Lucky instead of a Sweet," urged
a 1928 ad for Lucky Strikes. The deceptive message, that
smoking helps women stay slim and attractive, is one
that survives today.

Smoking rates for Americans—men as well as
women—soared over the following decades. During
World War II, soldiers received free cigarettes in their
ration cartons. With millions of American men serving
in the armed forces, women entered the workforce on
the home front, keeping the country's factories running.
Like the soldiers overseas, many women began smoking
during the war years to relieve the stress and monotony

of their lives. By the time the war ended in 1945, millions more Americans were addicted to tobacco.

By the mid-1950s, about one-quarter of all American women over twenty-one years of age were smokers,

Many tobacco companies started advertising specifically to women, as in this Lucky Strike poster.

according to estimates released by the National Institutes of Health. At the same time, more than half of all American men smoked.

The 1960s saw the rise of the feminist movement. Asserting that women in the United States continued to suffer second-class status, members of the movement

New brands and advertising specfically for women meant that more young girls started smoking as well; during the late 1960s there was a 110% increase in the number of 12-year-old girls who smoked.

demanded an end to discrimination based on gender, including the practice of paying male workers more money than their female counterparts in the same positions. As women demanding the right to vote had done earlier in the century, this new generation of feminists took to the streets, marching and demonstrating for equal rights.

The tobacco industry sensed an opportunity. It conducted market research studies on how best to sell cigarettes to a "more liberated" American woman.

Tennis and Cigarettes

Once again, tobacco companies created new brands and promotions for women. In many respects, the marketing mirrored earlier attempts to attract female smokers,

In the 1960s, the feminist movement gained popularity. Tobacco companies took advantage of this, selling cigarettes to these new, "liberated" women.

appealing to such traditional concerns as weight control, romance, sophistication, and relaxation. Cigarettes targeting women sometimes carried feminine scents and flavors, and the brand names, such as Silva Thins and Eve, also sounded feminine. Yet the new ad campaigns carried another message, one that was in tune with the

Sports and cigarettes became connected in people's minds, as tobacco companies started to sponsor sporting events, like this Virginia Slims tennis competition.

times: the idea of women smokers as independent, fun, and successful.

In 1968, the Philip Morris Company took this message a step further in introducing a new brand of women's cigarettes. "You've come a long way, baby," was the slogan for Virginia Slims, a long, slender cigarette. The ad campaign celebrated the feminist movement, equating Virginia Slims with independence and freedom. One ad showed a woman in old-fashioned dress hanging laundry, with the words, "Back then, every man gave his wife at least one day a week out of the house." The slogan equated women's rights and women's liberation with cigarettes.

Philip Morris soon found an excellent means of publicizing the Virginia Slims brand. During the late 1960s, women's professional tennis was struggling. Female players received low pay and poor recognition compared with men on the tennis circuit. Gladys Heldman, a tennis player and founder of *World Tennis* magazine, approached Philip Morris and suggested that Virginia Slims would benefit from partnering with women's tennis. In September 1970, Virginia Slims sponsored a women's tournament in Houston. The following year, the Virginia Slims tennis circuit got off the ground with tournaments around the country. With the cigarette company's backing, women's tennis took off. Top players, such as Billie Jean King, began earning substantial prize money. While women's tennis reaped huge benefits, the sponsorship gave Virginia Slims a previously untapped—or at least underused—advertising resource. Promotions for tennis matches featured Virginia Slims. Tennis stadiums displayed Virginia Slims ads, which were seen nationwide during televised events.

Kraft Foods, a Philip Morris subsidiary, eventually replaced Virginia Slims as the women's tennis sponsor. By 1990, however, the cigarette brand was in the midst of a new sort of campaign, again adapting its message to suit the changing times. That year, Virginia Slims launched a series of ads, each showing a woman from a different ethnic group. The slogan "Find your voice," with the tagline "No single institution owns the copyright for beauty," sent the message that young women of every culture had a right to smoke.

"A Full-Blown Epidemic"

With new brands and cigarette promotions for women, the numbers of female teenagers who took up smoking

Companies portrayed woman smokers as glamorous, beautiful, and sexy, trying to make cigarettes appealing for women of all kinds.

soared between 1967 and 1973, according to researchers at the Moores Cancer Center at the University of California, San Diego. In a report published in the *Journal of the American Medical Association*, the researchers found a 110 percent increase in start-up rates for twelve-year-old girls, a 55 percent increase among thirteen-year-old girls, and a 35 percent increase among seventeen-year-old girls during those years.

Along with the freedom to smoke came the risks. The Centers for Disease Control and Prevention (CDC) estimated that, between 1995 and 1999, 178,000 women died each year from smoking-related diseases. The women died on average 14.5 years earlier than their life expectancy, the CDC said.

In 2001, the Surgeon General's office released the report *Women and Smoking*. It confirmed the growing health crisis brought about by cigarette smoking among girls and women. By 2000, almost 30 percent of female high school seniors said they had smoked within the past month, according to the Surgeon General.

Smoking's harmful effects on women are appalling. Since the late 1980s, lung cancer has killed more women than any other cancer, including breast cancer. Heart disease, the leading killer of women, is exacerbated by smoking; about one in five of all deaths from heart disease among women is linked to smoking. Smoking can also harm women's reproductive systems, decreasing production of the female hormone estrogen and impairing fertility by affecting ovulation. In turn, smoking increases the risk of *osteoporosis* and other conditions affected by the level of estrogen.

Women who smoke while pregnant may harm the health of their fetus. Smoking by expectant mothers can slow fetal development and is linked to higher rates of *stillbirth* and *miscarriage*. But the risks don't end after a baby is delivered. Children exposed to secondhand smoke have a higher incidence of sudden infant death syndrome, or SIDS.

The enormity of the problem of women and smoking is undeniable. It was spelled out in a 2001 report by Surgeon General David Satcher:

> When calling attention to public health problems, we must not misuse the word "epidemic." But there is no better word to describe the 600 percent

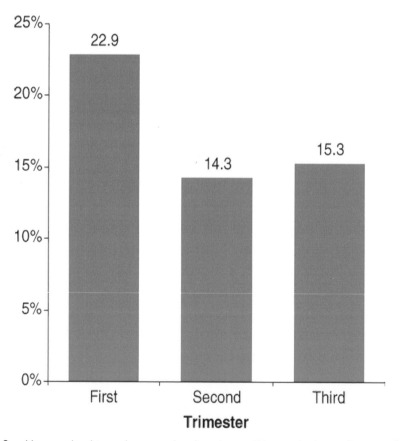

Smoking can lead to an increase in micarriages; this graph shows the rate of miscarriage during each trimester.

increase since 1950 in women's death rates for lung cancer, a disease primarily caused by smoking. Clearly, smoking-related disease among women is a full-blown epidemic.

The report criticized the tobacco industry for equating smoking with "women's freedom, emancipation, and empowerment."

By this time, a backlash against the tobacco industry's marketing practices had already been felt.   For example, in early 1990, R. J. Reynolds was set to roll out Dakota. This new brand targeted women—and specifically, younger women with low income and education levels. A promotional campaign was planned, with ads of young women on motorcycles. However, news of the campaign leaked out, spurring a public outcry. In the face of rising concern that young women should not be encouraged to smoke, the cigarette brand was discontinued.

Magazine Advertising and Young People

The Master Settlement Agreement of 1998 banned cigarette marketing that targeted children and youth under age eighteen. However, there appeared to be a significant loophole in the MSA: tobacco companies continued to advertise in magazines read by adults as well as youth, such as *Newsweek* and *Sports Illustrated*. In fact, studies showed that ads for cigarette brands popular with adolescents were much more likely to appear in publications with high youth readership than were ads for adult-oriented brands. Their promises notwithstanding, the cigarette manufacturers still seemed to be delib-

Tobacco manufacturers advertised their products in magazines, especially those aimed at younger readers, in an attempt to gain more customers.

erately marketing their products to young people.

To respond to this problem, the National Association of Attorneys General came to an agreement with cigarette companies and several magazines read by young people, including *Time*, *Newsweek*, *Sports Illustrated*, and *People*. Under the agreement, tobacco advertisements were pulled from school and library editions of the magazines. By 2007, many magazines had stopped running tobacco ads altogether.

Tobacco companies also scaled back print advertising overall. Philip Morris USA stopped advertising in newspapers and magazines in 2005, choosing to focus instead on direct marketing and in-store promotions. In fact, the budget for cigarette media advertising fell from $932 million in 1985 to $56 million in 2005, according to *Advertising Age*, an industry magazine.

Still, cigarette ads appeared periodically. A 2007 issue of *Rolling Stone* magazine displayed a full-page ad for Camels on the back cover. *Rolling Stone* is a pop culture icon, covering entertainment, music, politics, and television in ways that are interesting to young people. According to *Rolling Stone*'s 2006 media kit, 43 percent of the magazine's readers are between the ages of twelve and twenty-four, the age group most likely to start smoking.

Along with promotions in magazines, Camel No. 9 was launched at special parties in early 2007. A newspaper in Portland, Oregon, reported on a typical party; it included giveaways like berry lip balm, cell phone jewelry, and "rocker girl" wristbands.

At a Senate hearing that spring, legislators criticized the campaign. Senator Sherrod Brown, a Democrat from Ohio, displayed a Camel No. 9 flyer mailed to smokers. "It strains the imagination to think this campaign is aimed at anybody other than 15-, 16-, 17-year-old girls—something that's pretty morally repugnant," Brown told National Public Radio.

In June 2007, thirty-eight members of Congress sent a letter to women's magazines, including *Elle*, *Glamour*, *InStyle*, and *Us Weekly*, asking them to stop carrying tobacco ads. The letter read: "To our great concern, R. J. Reynolds is heavily relying on leading women's

Many tobacco companies aimed their products at teenage girls.

magazines, including yours, to aggressively market this deadly product to young women, including teenagers."

Health advocates and other smoking critics have worked diligently to curtail cigarette advertising in publications, especially those targeting youth and females. However, the promotion of smoking is of equal concern in other venues, including movies.

CHAPTER 4

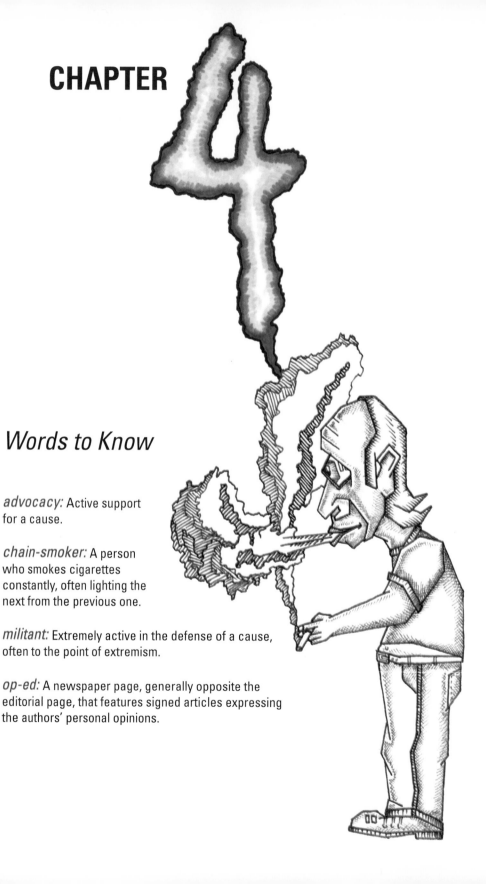

Words to Know

advocacy: Active support for a cause.

chain-smoker: A person who smokes cigarettes constantly, often lighting the next from the previous one.

militant: Extremely active in the defense of a cause, often to the point of extremism.

op-ed: A newspaper page, generally opposite the editorial page, that features signed articles expressing the authors' personal opinions.

Smoke on the Silver Screen

"Nobody really smokes anymore, or so it seems," reporter Carla Meyer noted in a *San Francisco Chronicle* story. "If they do, they're huddled against the cold, having been banished from their offices and forced to endure the dirty looks of passers-by. Yet onscreen, especially in the current holiday movies, people are puffing like it's 1959."

Meyer cited some well-received movies that featured characters smoking, including *The Royal Tenenbaums*, *Vanilla Sky*, and *In the Bedroom*. Meyer's story about smoking and motion pictures was from December 2001, but it could have been published in almost any recent year. Popular films continue to be filled with depictions of tobacco use.

Among the few places where smoking remains socially acceptable is in the world of entertainment. A 2002 study by the Office of National Drug Control Policy found that 21 percent of music videos feature cigarette smoking. While network television has curtailed on-camera smoking since the 1970s, some shows continue to include characters who smoke. In 2007, for example, the CW television network premiered the teen drama *Gossip Girl*, based on the book series by Cecily von Ziegesar, in which teens casually smoke while socializing. In addition, cable channels continue to air shows with smokers.

For antismoking activists, depictions of smoking on film are of particular concern because movies reach millions of viewers, including young people. Smoking has always been part of the Hollywood film industry, even in movies for young audiences. In 2007, new films with smoking scenes included *Ocean's Thirteen*, rated PG-13, and the popular R-rated film *Knocked Up*. Films released to DVD during 2007 also included characters who smoke, such as *Ghost Rider* (PG-13) and the DreamWorks comedy *Norbit*. Smoking hasn't always been taboo even in animated films aimed at young children. In the Disney classic *101 Dalmatians*, for example, the villain, Cruella De Vil, carries a scarlet cigarette holder. Often it's the villain who smokes. But glamorous, heroic, and sympathetic main characters also light up.

"A teen going to the movies today will leave with the misimpression that smoking is widely accepted—that is, the 'winners' smoke, and no health or social consequences are associated with smoking," wrote Stanton A. Glantz, director of the Center for Tobacco Control Research and Education, in a medical journal editorial in 2002. A leading tobacco industry critic, Glantz founded

Even animated movies often have smoking in them, like Cruella De Vil in the film, *101 Dalmations.*

Many movie stars in the 1930s and 1940s made no attempt to hide the fact that they smoked. Here, Humphrey Bogart smokes a cigarette.

Smoke Free Movies, an *advocacy* group to reduce tobacco use in films.

Golden Age of Movies and Cigarettes

Smoking played a big role in the golden age of Hollywood. Male and female stars smoked copiously in films of the 1930s and 1940s. Cigarettes and cigars served as props to emphasize character and mood. One of the most famous images in film history was created when Marlene Dietrich lit a cigarette in the dark in the 1932 classic Shanghai Express. Her character was supposed to be traveling by train through China during a raging civil war, and the scene became an emblem of glamour, romance, and intrigue.

Another classic in which on-screen smoking figured prominently was 1942's *Casablanca*. Set in North Africa during World War II, the drama—which appears on many critics' lists of greatest movies of all time—won the Academy Award for Best Picture in 1943. Its romantic leads, Ingrid Bergman

Bright Leaf

In Caswell County, North Carolina, in 1839, an eighteen-year-old slave named Stephen tried something new to cure tobacco. He had to do something. Stephen had fallen asleep, and the wood fire he was using to cure tobacco went out. The wood had gotten damp, and he couldn't get another fire going. So Stephen used charcoal to cure the tobacco. It made a lighter-colored and -flavored tobacco than when wood was used.

The leaves produced in this area were known as Piedmont. They were already a lighter color than the Virginia-grown leaf because they were grown in a lighter-colored soil. The combination of the light golden-colored leaf and the lighter curing method produced tobacco called "Bright Leaf." This new tobacco was the mildest of all tobaccos to smoke.

and Humphrey Bogart, smoked continually. So did the supporting characters. "Ten people light up during the film. And characters are seen smoking thirty-one different times—a pack and a half in just 101 minutes," wrote popular culture historian Jack Nachbar in the *Journal of Popular Film and Television*. "Even in an era when smoking was common in the movies, *Casablanca*'s characters have unusually heavy habits."

Historically, smoking was portrayed in movies and popular culture as glamorous; it was something that all the movie stars did.

Like many stars of the era, Bergman and Bogart were smokers off-screen as well. So, too, was actor Ronald Reagan, who appeared in ads for Chesterfield cigarettes during the 1940s and 1950s. Reagan would go on to become the fortieth president of the United States.

The Hollywood classics, like contemporary films, did not show smoking's negative aspects, such as the bad breath, yellowed teeth, and coughing. And at the time, the long-term health effects weren't widely known. Over the years, however, many of Hollywood's biggest stars would pay a huge price for their smoking habit. Bogart died of cancer of the esophagus in 1957. Gary Cooper, a two-time Academy Award winner, succumbed to lung cancer in 1961. Glamorous actress Betty Grable died of lung cancer in 1973. Western movies icon John Wayne was stricken with the same disease. Before his death in 1979, Wayne did a commercial for the American Cancer Society. Yul Brynner, star of film classics such as *The King and I* and *The Magnificent Seven*, also did an antismoking commercial, which aired *after* his death from lung cancer in 1985. "Now that I'm gone, I tell you, don't smoke," the actor advised. "Whatever you do, just don't smoke. If I could take back that smoking, we wouldn't be talking about any cancer. I'm convinced of that." Brynner's commercial can be viewed on the Web site of the Yul Brynner Head and Neck Cancer Foundation.

Effects on Teen Viewers

Smoking in American movies "reached historic heights" in 2002, states a report by the Center for Tobacco Control Research and Education. The center surveyed all films released to theaters between 1998 and 2006. Researchers found that 75 percent of these films featured tobacco use. That figure includes 88 percent of R-rated films, 75 percent of PG-13 movies, and 36 percent of G/PG movies. After their theatrical run, many of these movies later appeared on television or were released as DVDs, thereby gaining an even wider audience.

The fact that movies popular with young people still feature characters who smoke concerns health experts and antismoking advocates.

Recipe for Success

The formula for chewing tobacco was a guarded secret in each factory making it in the 1830s. Lists of ingredients may have given the impression that cake, rather than a tobacco product, was being made. The tobacco was soaked in vats of flavorings before it was pressed into molds. Most chewing tobacco included a sweetener such as molasses, sugar, or honey. Some contained up to 25 percent sugar. Sweeteners were combined with flavors such as licorice, rum, nutmeg, tonka beans, cinnamon, almond oil, lemon, cardamom, mace, caraway, and fennel seed.

Chewing tobacco had masculine-sounding brand names such as Live and Let Live, Buzz Saw, Barbed Wire, Bull of the Woods, and Cannon Ball.

"Smoking in movies is a major and growing health problem," Glantz wrote in the scientific journal *Lancet* in 2002. Glantz has urged the film industry to stop showing smoking. "Every day of delay means more unnecessary addiction and death because of Hollywood's love affair with the tobacco industry," he asserted.

Studies have shown that exposure to smoking in films can encourage teens to smoke. Teenagers who watch a lot of movies with characters who smoke tend to smoke more than teens who don't watch as many of those movies, according to researchers at Dartmouth Medical

School. The researchers reported, in the medical journal *Pediatrics*, that thirty-eight of every one hundred young people who tried cigarettes did so because they saw smoking in the movies.

Tobacco critics say casual smoking in films can imply that smoking is glamorous and exciting. When popular movie stars, from Julia Roberts to Johnny Depp, smoke on-screen, teens may want to imitate their behavior. Young movie viewers are likely aware of the risks, but the more they see smoking on-screen, the more desirable and attractive smoking can become, experts say. If teens see smoking in movies as a natural part of everyday life, health warnings aren't as effective.

In the past, tobacco companies, like other companies with products to sell, paid to place their products in movies. For example, Philip Morris paid Warner Brothers to feature Marlboros on-screen over twenty times in the 1980 blockbuster *Superman II*.

Many teenagers started smoking in order to be like their favorite movie star.

In 1980, Philip Morris made sure their product appeared in the movie Superman II, when they paid Warner Brohters to feature Marlboro; many critics disagree with these tactics, saying that portraying smoking on screen only encourages people to smoke.

In plenty of cases, however, filmmakers included smoking in their movies without any monetary incentives from the tobacco industry. "I do feel heartened at the increasing number of occasions when I go to a movie and see a pack of cigarettes in the hands of the leading lady," declared Hamish Maxwell, president of Philip Morris, in a 1983 marketing speech. "This is in sharp contrast to the state of affairs just a few years ago when cigarettes rarely showed up on camera. We must continue to exploit new opportunities to get cigarettes on screen and into the hands of smokers." (The speech is one of many corporate documents available to the public at the Web site tobaccodocuments.org.)

In 1989, under pressure from Congress, tobacco companies agreed to a voluntary ban on paying to place cigarette brands in movies. The MSA of 1998 went a step further, specifically prohibiting tobacco companies from paying to promote tobacco products in movies, television, theater, videos, and video games. Despite the restrictions, tobacco did not disappear from the silver screen.

Who's Responsible?

The decision to include cigarettes in a movie can happen during any stage of a film's development. Actor Kirk Douglas recalled that he first lit up a cigarette after a director instructed him to do so for a scene. Douglas was playing the husband of Barbara Stanwyck, another screen legend, in the 1946 film *The Strange Loves of Martha Ivers*. Before he knew it, Douglas was smoking two or three packs a day. "At that time everyone smoked, and the cigarette was the favorite movie prop," the actor wrote in a *New York Times' op-ed*. "Hollywood started me smoking, literally putting a cigarette in my hand. Who knows how many moviegoers have started smoking because of what they have seen on the screen? Too many movies glorify young people smoking. It doesn't have to be this way."

The screenwriter is often the person who directs a character to light up a cigarette. In 2002, Hollywood

Children who see smoking in video games or movies are more likely to think that it's okay to smoke themselves.

screenwriter Joe Eszterhas, recently diagnosed with throat cancer, issued a public apology for glamorizing cigarettes in his blockbusters, such as 1992's *Basic Instinct*. "I've written 14 movies, and in many of them, people were smoking, and heroes were smoking. I was a *militant* smoker, and in my case, I think I particularly used smoking because what I felt was a kind of politically correct big brother assault on smoking," he told CNN anchor Paula Zahn. After being treated for cancer and meeting other cancer patients, Eszterhas had become "haunted" by the thought that he may have encouraged people to engage in smoking. He wrote in the *New York Times*:

> A cigarette in the hands of a Hollywood star on screen is a gun aimed at a 12- or 14-year-old. The gun will go off when the kid is an adult. We in Hollywood know the gun will go off, yet we hide behind a smokescreen of phrases like creative freedom and artistic freedom. Those lofty words are lies designed at best to obscure laziness. I know, I have told those lies.

Not everyone in Hollywood accepts smoking in films. Actor and director Rob Reiner, for example, has been waging an antismoking crusade for years. He and several other leaders in the entertainment industry started Hollywood Unfiltered, a campaign that's part of the Entertainment Industry Foundation. Supported by the Screen Actors Guild and other industry groups, Hollywood Unfiltered seeks to educate the film industry on the dangers to young people of on-screen smoking and to get cigarettes off movie screens.

First Amendment

Many people question whether it is fair—or even legal under the First Amendment, which protects free speech—to ban smoking in films. Films try to capture real life, and cigarettes are a fact of life, particularly of historical eras such as World War II or the 1950s. Many people believe that prohibiting smoking is censorship and places unfair limits on artistic freedom. The late Jack Valenti, longtime president of the Motion Picture Association of America (MPAA), spoke out strongly against restrictions. "Smoking by some actors is essential to the time and place of the story, and is indispensable to quickly identify the actor's demeanor and character to advance the narrative, and then no one ought to intervene in a director's design for telling his story the way he chooses to tell it," Valenti told the Senate Commerce Committee in 2002. Many in Hollywood fear that a smoking ban might lead to other restrictions on film content.

Other countries have tried a ban on depictions of smoking. In 2005, India banned smoking in movies and on television. India's popular Bollywood film industry opposed the ban. Indian film director Shekhar Kapur said the ban could lead to other efforts to censor creativity. "The Indian government has always thought themselves able to do whatever they feel is necessary to curtail artistic freedoms," Kapur told CNN. "The fear is not that we have to stop showing people smoking. The fear is that this is the beginning of a series of bans."

The Indian health minister disagreed, saying the ban would "protect the lives of millions of children who could be addicted to smoking under the influence of movies." India has some 250 million smokers, according to World Health Organization estimates, and more than

Jack Valenti, longtime president of the MPAA, spoke out strongly against banning smoking in films.

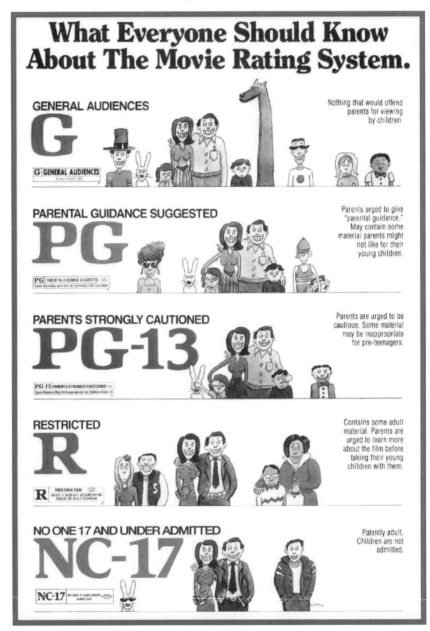

Today, some people argue that smoking should be considered when rating movies. However, no such standards have been put in place yet.

800,000 people in the country die from smoking-related illnesses each year.

The Film Ratings System and Smoking

Since 1968, the MPAA has voluntarily rated movies according to their suitability to be viewed by young people. The ratings are supposed to help parents decide whether to allow their children to see a particular movie. Films that contain nothing that might be inappropriate for a child receive a G rating. At the other end of the spectrum is the NC-17 rating. It signifies that the film contains elements such as extreme depictions of violence, graphic sex, pervasive drug abuse, or aberrant behavior, and no one under the age of seventeen is permitted to see the movie in a theater. The most commercially successful movies tend to carry ratings of PG-13 (meaning that some material may be unsuitable for children under thirteen years of age) or R (meaning that youth under age seventeen must be accompanied by an adult to see the movie, which may contain considerable violence, nudity and sexual content, profane language, or depictions of drug abuse).

In 2007, a group of states attorneys general wrote letters to film industry leaders, requesting that a new element be considered in assigning film ratings: smoking. Under pressure, the MPAA decided that the ratings board would consider smoking as one of several factors in

The classic movie "tough guy" image.

rating films. In a press statement, MPAA chairman Dan Glickman stated:

> Clearly, smoking is increasingly an unacceptable behavior in our society. There is broad awareness of smoking as a unique public health concern due to nicotine's highly addictive nature, and no parent wants their child to take up the habit. The appropriate response of the rating system is to give more information to parents on this issue.

However, the MPAA balked at giving films an R rating just because they contained smoking. Instead, the ratings board planned to note in movie descriptions that the film glamorized smoking or contained pervasive smoking. In the future, fewer movies for children and teen audiences will likely include a famous actor lighting up a cigarette.

Some production companies are already taking greater care when deciding whether to include cigarettes in films expected to be viewed by young people. In the summer of 2007, Disney became the first major studio to ban smoking from its family movies. No smoking would occur in Disney-branded films, and smoking would be reduced in Miramax and Touchstone films, also owned by the company. "This is good for the perception of Disney, but the primary reason is that cigarette smoking is a hazard and we should avoid depicting it in movies and on television," Robert A. Iger, Disney's chief executive, told a *New York Times* reporter.

On the small screen, the Hallmark television channel planned to follow Disney's lead.

Disney has gotten rid of all smoking in its movies and has decreased the amount of smoking seen in movies produced by the other studios it owns.

Tobacco companies have spent years, and countless dollars, bombarding American youth with pro-smoking messages. In recent years, teens who have taken charge of their own health have been striking back. One way they do this is through antismoking campaigns that reach out to their peers.

CHAPTER 5

Words to Know

bias: An unreasonable personal preference; an opinion that isn't supported by facts.

grassroots: Involving ordinary people in a community or an organization.

Smartening Up: Teens Get Real About Tobacco

Blue outlines of bodies were spread over the floors of Drury High School in North Adams, Massachusetts, on a spring day in 2007. Members of Students Against Second-hand Smoking in Youth (SASSY), an antismoking group, drew the outlines to represent the number of deaths caused by smoking. They also posted information about the dangers of tobacco on bulletin boards and in hallways, and put magnets reading "Smoking-Cool? NOT" on lockers.

Teen activists are a growing force against smoking. Anti-smoking campaigns spearheaded by teens have spread across the country. Young people are taking this health issue into their own hands, trying to convince their peers to say no to

Today, there are many different campaigns that are teaching teens how to say no to tobacco.

cigarettes. Many groups use media campaigns to send their messages. From Internet Web sites to videos, as well as *grassroots* events like the one in North Adams, groups try to reach their peers in ways that will make them listen. Just as cigarette ads of the past tried to lure people with promises of being cool, hip, and smart, the new antismoking campaigns try to capture teens' attention and sway their behavior. This time, however, the message is to stop smoking, not start. "All I want is for one person to not start smoking. I want one person to quit," said one SASSY member in an interview with iBerkshires.com, a community news Web site.

Truth Campaign

The 1998 MSA required tobacco companies to pay for antismoking ads, education, and tobacco information. The agreement also called for the funding and creation of a national organization to fight smoking. Begun in 1999, the American Legacy Foundation, located in Washington, D.C., has helped develop national programs to address the health effects of tobacco. These programs range from tobacco research to community education. Steered by a board made up of leaders in medicine, law, politics, and higher education, the foundation focuses on educating young people on the hazards of smoking, and reducing inequalities in the public's access to tobacco education and smoking-cessation programs. The foundation also takes stands on current tobacco issues. In 2007, the foundation came out against the Camel No. 9 ad campaign.

In 2000, the American Legacy Foundation launched the "Truth" campaign to stop young people from smoking. According to several studies, the campaign's edgy ads helped contribute to the downward trend in youth smoking seen in the first years of the twenty-first century. One ad shows a cowboy riding his horse through New York City traffic. He takes off his neckerchief to reveal a hole in his neck, while singing a song that starts, "You don't always die from tobacco; sometimes you just lose a lung." In a foundation survey, almost 90 percent of teens who saw the "Truth" ads said they were convincing; 85 percent said the ads gave them reasons to not smoke.

The tobacco settlement also provided states with funding to set up antismoking programs for young people. South Carolina started a popular antismoking program, Rage Against the Haze, in 2000. The program began as a Web site, but soon it expanded into a grassroots campaign, drawing teens from around the state to become active in antismoking efforts. In Colorado, Get R!EAL (Resist! Expose Advertising Lies), a teen antismoking group, set up a Web site with lots of good information

World's Rarest Baseball Card

Honus Wagner was a shortstop for the Pittsburgh Pirates baseball team from 1900 to 1917. In 1909 he didn't want his picture on a cigarette trading card produced by the American Tobacco Company. Why he felt that way has been debated for many years. Some claim it was because Wagner was a non-smoker and didn't want to set a bad example for children. According to the Baseball Hall of Fame, however, Wagner was a smoker but didn't want children to have to buy tobacco products to get his card. Whatever the reason, he ordered the American Tobacco Company to remove his picture from its cards.

Because few Honus Wagner cards were produced, the card became the most valuable baseball card of all time. Only fifty to sixty of the cards exist today. A 1909 Honus Wagner card sold for $2.35 million in 2007!

on smoking and the media. In Virginia, the Y Street Web site provides advice for teens on how to take antismoking action on the local level. Washington State's health department sponsors a Web site, www.seethroughthesmoke.com, with lots of eye-opening, disturbing facts about smoking.

The Internet has blossomed into a popular medium for spreading the antismoking message. Trying to reach teens who spend their free time surfing the Internet, Massachusetts created an antismoking Web site, the84.org. The number 84 is the percentage of Massachusetts teens in grades seven through twelve who do not smoke. Thus, teens learn that most of their peers are nonsmokers, and they should join the crowd. With catchy graphics and easy navigation, the Web site provides startling

Rage Against the Haze is a grassroots campaign to stop teen smoking in South Carolina.

Today, many anti-smoking campaigns are using computers and the Internet to reach a broader audience.

facts, such as: "Smoke got you broke? Smoking a pack of cigarettes a day can cost over $2,000 a year. That's worth over 8 MP3 players, 5 cell phones, or 2,000 music downloads." Teens also blog about their smoking experiences and see how others cope with similar problems.

Teen antismoking campaigns like the one in Massachusetts have been effective. However, most states have limited budgets for health education. Antismoking campaigns often run up against funding troubles, and some states have been forced to cut back in recent years. In 2000, Minnesota started a teen antismoking campaign, Target Market, using tobacco settlement funding. One of the ads said:

> I just want to say thank you. Thanks. Thank you Big Tobacco, for convincing me to smoke. And this filter just makes me feel so safe. Thanks. It's like a seat belt or an air bag. Thank you Big Tobacco for singling me out as a main target. For underestimating our intelligence. Thanks a lot.

When Minnesota cut the program's funding in 2004 to help balance the state budget, a study by the CDC showed that teens immediately became more likely to start smoking. "This study shows that cutting back on these programs not only turns the clock back on our successful efforts to cut back on youth smoking, but does so quickly and dramatically," commented Cass Wheeler, chief executive officer of the American Heart Association.

Tobacco Company Campaigns

Tobacco companies fund their own antismoking campaigns to discourage children and teens from taking

Today, there are many varied campaigns that fight to keep kids and young adults from starting to smoke.

up the habit. Several large companies discuss smoking hazards on their Web sites. The Philip Morris USA Web site offers information on how parents can raise kids who don't smoke. Like other companies, Philip Morris states that adults should be free to choose whether to smoke, but young people should be encouraged never to start. The R. J. Reynolds site says minors should never use tobacco products, and adults who do not use

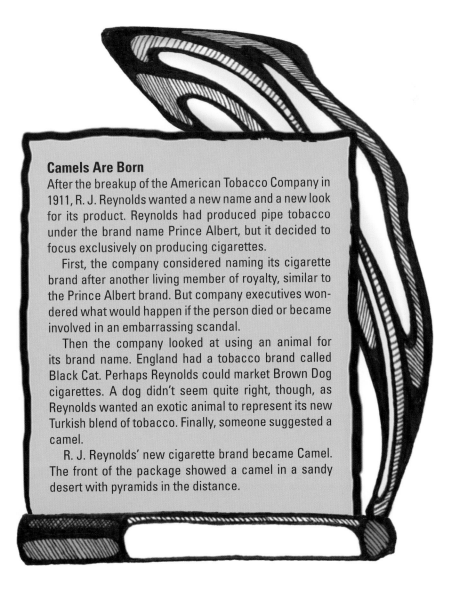

Camels Are Born

After the breakup of the American Tobacco Company in 1911, R. J. Reynolds wanted a new name and a new look for its product. Reynolds had produced pipe tobacco under the brand name Prince Albert, but it decided to focus exclusively on producing cigarettes.

First, the company considered naming its cigarette brand after another living member of royalty, similar to the Prince Albert brand. But company executives wondered what would happen if the person died or became involved in an embarrassing scandal.

Then the company looked at using an animal for its brand name. England had a tobacco brand called Black Cat. Perhaps Reynolds could market Brown Dog cigarettes. A dog didn't seem quite right, though, as Reynolds wanted an exotic animal to represent its new Turkish blend of tobacco. Finally, someone suggested a camel.

R. J. Reynolds' new cigarette brand became Camel. The front of the package showed a camel in a sandy desert with pyramids in the distance.

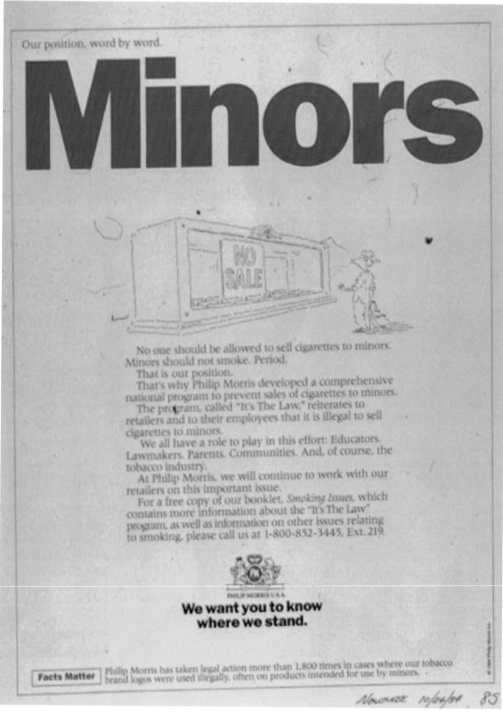

The government has cracked down on the consumption of tobacco by minors; this includes a stiff fine for anyone who sells cigarettes or chewing tobacco to anyone under the age of 18.

or have quit using tobacco products should not start. The site contains a page titled "For Adults Who Choose to Use Tobacco . . . Smoking & Health Issues." The page states:

> R. J. Reynolds Tobacco Company believes smoking causes serious disease and is addictive. No tobacco product has been shown to be safe, and individuals should rely on the conclusions of the U.S. Surgeon General, the Centers for Disease Control and other public health and medical officials when making decisions regarding smoking.

Not everyone agrees that the tobacco companies' antismoking efforts are effective, however. In fact, some studies suggest that tobacco company antismoking ad campaigns can do more harm than good. Stanford University researchers studied a group of California high school students who watched smoking-prevention ads sponsored by tobacco companies and others created by the American Legacy Foundation. Both sets of ads had similar effects on the students' intentions to smoke, but the tobacco company ads helped to promote their corporate image and gave the students a more favorable view of the industry. "By cultivating public opinion that is more sympathetic toward tobacco companies, the effect of such advertising is likely to be more harmful than helpful to youth," states the study, which was published in 2006 in the journal *Tobacco Control*.

The most straightforward accounts of smoking's health effects often work best. After ABC news anchor Peter Jennings died of lung cancer in 2005, his former news program, *World News Tonight*, aired a series about people trying to quit smoking. The series, *Quit to Live:*

Fighting Lung Cancer, broadcast the number for a national quit line, which connected callers to counselors in their states. During the series, the number of calls to the quit line tripled, evidence that the public's shock at the death of Jennings, coupled with health information presented during the broadcast, increased smokers' desire to take action about their health. Soon after the series ended, however, the call rate fell again.

Media Literacy

American teens are surrounded by consumer products and promises on television, in magazines, and at the movies. Most antismoking programs try to alert teens and adults to become smarter about tobacco and other products in the media. Teens must learn to see through the media images in order to make good decisions. Known as media literacy, this set of skills is being taught today in schools across the country. A common definition of media literacy is the ability to access, analyze, evaluate, and communicate information in many formats. To do this, people use higher-level thinking skills to question, analyze, and understand information and images from television, movies, music, the Internet, books, newspapers, and other media.

For example, when watching a commercial, a teen might ask questions such as: What is the targeted audience? What values are being promoted? What is the message? Does the commercial appeal to me, and why? By asking these questions, a young person can decide whether to accept the message or reject it. When it comes to tobacco marketing, teens can learn to analyze the images and spot *bias*, misinformation, or even lies. They can also identify what information is left out. By using their knowledge, experience, and values, teens can draw their own conclusions.

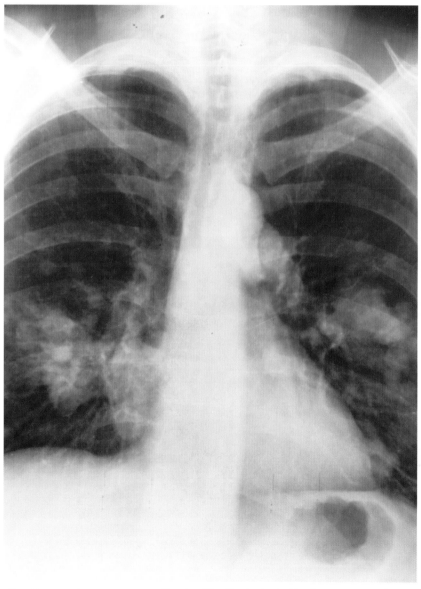

Smoking can have many negative health effects, including lung cancer, shown here. Many campaigns are attempting to advertise these health effects to teens, who may be pressured to start smoking.

Media literacy is one of the ways teens can protect themselves from tobacco, according to a 2006 study by researchers at the University of Pittsburgh School of Medicine. "Many factors that influence a teen's decision to smoke, like peer influence, parental smoking and risk-seeking tendency, are difficult to change," said lead author Dr. Brian Primack, assistant professor at the School of Medicine, in a statement on the school's Web site. "However, media literacy, which can be taught, may be a valuable tool in efforts to discourage teens from smoking."

Percentages of Cancers Caused by Smoking

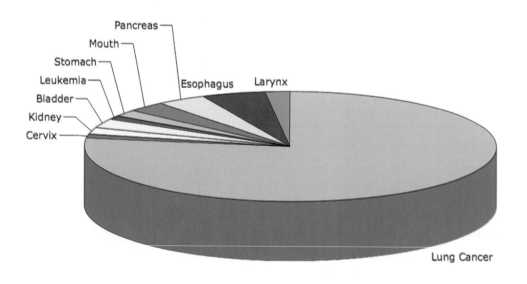

This chart shows that 78% of the cancer caused by smoking is lung cancer.

Making Decisions

Teen smoking rates fell during the 1990s, but the decline came to a standstill after 2002, according to the CDC and other health watchdog organizations. One reason, experts say, may be that fewer antismoking media campaigns were being funded. Cutbacks for state antismoking programs and the American Legacy Foundation's national "Truth" campaign reduced the number of smoking-cessation media campaigns. Also, price increases in cigarettes began to level off, creating less of a deterrent for teens with limited dollars to spend.

"The decline in teen smoking seems to be about over," Lloyd Johnston, a social psychologist at the University of Michigan, told National Public Radio in 2007. Johnston has surveyed teens about tobacco for more than three decades. "We didn't see any decline in daily smoking among the eighth-graders this year, and they're usually the first to show changes in direction. And the declines have decelerated considerably in 10th and 12th grade as well."

Meanwhile, new challenges lie ahead for teens trying to navigate the media and stay away from tobacco. Tobacco advertising is prohibited on the Internet, and the major American tobacco companies do not sell cigarettes on their Web sites. Still, at least one major tobacco company has a Web site apart from its corporate site, where adults over age twenty-one can sign up to receive coupons and special offers. In fact, a simple Google search for "cigarettes" turns up hundreds, if not thousands, of Web sites with names like "cheap cigarettes" or "discount cigarettes." These sites are mostly run by independent cigarette retailers, but they sell well-known brands. And with a few keystrokes, a consumer can fill a virtual cart with cigarettes and order with a credit card number. While the sites prohibit shoppers who are not adults, this might not stop teens determined to get cigarettes.

Whether surfing the Internet, watching a favorite movie star light up a cigarette, or encountering a cigarette ad at a local convenience store, teens must make decisions about what they see on a daily basis. As the

The Internet can be an important medium for spreading the truth about smoking.

Massachusetts antismoking teen Web site the84.org states:

> We've got the skills to be aware and critical of Big Tobacco. We've got the power and ability to share that knowledge with other young people—and rob Big Tobacco of their future customers. We're into a lot of things that beat smoking. We're The 84 and growing.

Filtering through the images and figuring out what to do is a teen's constant challenge. The more information teens have, the better able they will be to make good decisions.

Further Reading

Balkin, Karen, and Helen Cothran. *Tobacco and Smoking (Opposing Viewpoints Series)*. San Diego, Calif.: Greenhaven Press, 2004.

Covey, Sean. *The 6 Most Important Decisions You'll Ever Make: A Guide for Teens*. New York: Simon and Schuster, 2006.

Hernandez, Roger E. *Teens and the Media*. Broomall, Pa.: Mason Crest Publishers, 2005.

Heyes, Eileen. *Tobacco U.S.A.: The Industry Behind the Smoke Curtain*. Minneapolis, Minn.: Twenty-First Century Books, 1999.

Hyde, Margaret O., and John F. Setaro. *Smoking 101: An Overview for Teens*, Minneapolis, Minn.: Twenty-First Century Books, 2006.

Moe, Barbara A. *Teen Smoking and Tobacco Use: A Hot Issue*. Berkeley Heights, N.J.: Enslow, 2000.

For More Information

The American Legacy Foundation
www.americanlegacy.org

Dangers of Tobacco
www.seethruthesmoke.com

Hollywood Unfiltered
hollywoodunfiltered.org

Massachusetts Teen Antismoking Web Site
the84.org/home/index.php?id=2

Media Literacy
pbskids.org/dontbuyit

Smoking at the Movies
smokefreemovies.ucsf.edu/problem/index.html

Smoking Facts
www.cdc.gov/tobacco

Teen Anti-Smoking Resources
www.notobacco.org

Publisher's note:
The Web sites listed on this page were active at the time of publication. The publisher is not responsible for Web sites that have changed their addresses or discontinued operation since the date of publication. The publisher will review and update the Web-site list upon each reprint.

Bibliography

Associated Press. "New Camel Brand Courts Women, Sparks Ire," May 3, 2007. *MSNBC.* http://www.msnbc.msn.com/id/18471378.

Atkinson, Claire. "Missing a Larynx, He's Become the Voice of Antismoking Efforts." *New York Times*, July 17, 2007.

Augustson, Erik. "Smoking Control. Impact of National ABC Promotion on 1-800-QUIT-NOW." *American Journal of Health Promotion* (July/August, 2007).

Barnes, Brooks. "Bowing to Pressure, Disney Bans Smoking in Its Branded Movies." *New York Times*, July 26, 2007.

Benson, Lorna. "Anti-Smoking Campaign Is Gone; Teen Smoking Is Up." *Minnesota Public Radio*, May 13, 2004. http://news.minnesota.publicradio.org/features/2004/05/13_bensonl_teensmoking.

Boliek, Brooks. "Valenti: Filtering Tobacco Smoking Is Filmmakers' Call." *Hollywood Reporter*, May 12, 2004.

Brand, Madeleine. "New York City Sees Decline in Smoking." *National Public Radio*, June 22, 2007. http://www.npr.org/templates/story/story.php?storyId=11277619.

Brandt, Allan M. *The Cigarette Century: The Rise, Fall, and Deadly Persistence of the Product That Defined America.* New York: Basic Books, 2007.

Charlesworth, Annemarie, and Stanton A. Glantz. "Smoking in the Movies Increases Adolescent Smoking: A Review." *Pediatrics* 116 (2005): 1516–1528.

CNN Access. *Joe Eszterhas Talks Hollywood Smoke Screen*, August 12, 2002. http://archives.cnn.com/2002/SHOWBIZ/Movies/08/12/eszterhas.cnna.

Dotinga, Randy. "National TV Promotion Triples Calls to Smoking Cessation Hotline." *Health Behavior News Service*, June 29, 2007. http://www.hbns.org/getDocument.cfm?documentID=1529.

Douglas, Kirk. "My First Cigarette, and My Last." *New York Times*, May 16, 2003.

Eszterhas, Joe. "Hollywood's Responsibility for Smoking Deaths." *New York Times*, August 9, 2002.

Federal Trade Commission. *Federal Trade Commission Cigarette Report for 2004 and 2005*, 2007. http://www.ftc.gov/reports/tobacco/2007cigarette2004-2005.pdf.

Fischer, P. M., et al. "Brand Logo Recognition by Children Aged 3 to 6 Years. Mickey Mouse and Old Joe the Camel." *Journal of American Medical Association* 266 (December 11, 1991). http://jama.ama-assn.org/cgi/content/abstract/266/22/3145.

Freeman, Becky. "USA: Not so Pretty in Pink." *Tobacco Control*, April 2007. http://espace.library.uq.edu.au/eserv.php?pid=UQ:13607&dsID=Freeman_no_so_pretty_in_pink.pdf.

Glantz, Stanton A., "Rate Movies with Smoking 'R'." *Effective Clinical Practice* 5 (January/February 2002): 31–34.

Henriksen, L., et al. "Industry Sponsored Anti-Smoking Ads and Adolescent Reactance: Test of a Boomerang Effect." *Tobacco Control* 15 (February 2006): 13–18.

Hochberg, Adam. "Critics Fume Over Marketing of Camel No. 9." *Morning Edition, National Public Radio,* March 16, 2007. http://www.npr.org/templates/story/story.php?storyId=8909745.

Johnson, Bradley. "Marlboro Man Rides into the Sunset." *Advertising Age,* June 25, 2007.

Juarez, Leo. "Bollywood Smoking Ban Sparks Controversy." *CNN,* June 28, 2005. http://www.cnn.com/2005/SHOWBIZ/Movies/06/27/bollywood.smoking/index.html.

Jussel, Amy. "Pink Dreams Turn to Ashes." *Shaping Youth,* January 2007. http://www.shapingyouth.org/blog/?m=200701.

Kaplan, Janice. "Can the New James Bond Measure Up?" *Parade Magazine,* October 1, 2006.

Kessler, David. *Question of Intent: A Great American Battle with a Deadly Industry.* New York: Public Affairs, 2001.

King, Charles, III, and Michael Siegel. "The Master Settlement Agreement with the Tobacco Industry and Cigarette Advertising in Magazines." *New England Journal of Medicine* 345 (2001): 504–511.

Kluger, Richard. *Ashes to Ashes: America's Hundred-Year Cigarette War, the Public Health, and the Unabashed Triumph of Philip Morris.* New York: Vintage Books, 1997.

Levin, Madeleine, and Diane Zuckerman. "Smoking Is a Woman's Issue." Issue Brief, National Research Center for Women and Families, May 2004. http://www.center4research.org/ibrief-05-04smoking.html.

Legacy Tobacco Documents Library, University of California, San Francisco. http://legacy.library.ucsf.edu.

Meyer, Carol. "Rising Up from the Ashtrays. Cigarettes Return to Films in a Big Way." *San Francisco Chronicle*, December 27, 2001.

Nachbar, Jack. "Doing the Thinking for All of Us: *Casablanca* and the Home Front." *Journal of Popular Film and Television* 27 (Winter 2000): 5–15.

Noveck, Jocelyn. "Camel No. 9: Is the Smartly Packaged Cigarette for Females Deft Marketing, or a Cynical Ploy?" *Sun Times*, May 4, 2007. http://www.suntimes.com/lifestyles/health/372084,camel050507.article.

Office of Public Affairs, University of Chicago Medical Center. *Cigarette Ads Target Youth, Violating $250 Billion 1998 Settlement.* http://www.uchospitals.edu/news/2002/20020312-tobacco.html.

"Parent Resource Center. Cigarette Smoking and Teens." Philip Morris USA. http://www.pmusa.com/en/prc/facts/smoking.asp.

Pierce, J. P., L. Lee, and E. A. Gilpin. "Smoking Initiation by Adolescent Girls, 1944 Through 1988. An Association with Targeted Advertising." *Journal of the American Medical Association* 271 (February 23, 1994): 608–611.

Rabin, Robert L., and Stephen D. Sugarman. *Regulating Tobacco.* New York: Oxford University Press, 2001.

Salkever, Alex. "Marlboro Man Lives," *Salon.* February 10, 2000. http://archive.salon.com/health/feature/2000/02/10/tobacco_ads/index1.html.

Sargent, J. D., et al. "Exposure to Movie Smoking: Its Relation to Smoking Initiation Among US Adolescents." *Pediatrics* 116 (2005): 1183–1191.

Smith, Stephen. "Where There's Smoke, Some See an 'R' Rating." *Boston Globe*, May 12, 2007.

Spencer, Lee. "Winston Made Cup What It Is." *Sporting News*, December 8, 2003.

U.S. Department of Health and Human Services. *Women and Smoking. A Report of the Surgeon General.* 2001. http://www.cdc.gov/tobacco/data_statistics/sgr/sgr_2001/index.htm.

Woody, Larry. "The End of Tobacco Road." *Auto Racing Digest*, December 2003.

Index

Picture Credits

Alcohol Tobacco and Tax: p. 40

Bureau of Census: p. 40

Creative Creative Commons Attribution 3.0
    Emmanuelm: p. 18

Dreamstime.com
    Amaviael: p. 100
    Andresr: p. 74
    Ckalt: p. 58
    Gvictoria: p. 34
    Icholakov: p. 71
    Ladyminnie: p. 22
    Mitarart: p. 54
    Moori: p. 90
    Wtolenaars: p. 60
    Zweig17: p. 80

istockphoto.com
    Stewart, Christian J.: p. 98

Jupiter Images: p. 46, 65

Motion Picture Association of America (MPAA), p.78

National Cancer Institute: p. 97
National Library of Medicine (NLM), profiles in Science: pp. 20, 32

Office of Applied Statistics: pp. 25, 56

Tobaccodocuments.org
    American Tobacco Co.: p. 49
    Brown & Williamson: p. 38
    Philip Morris: pp. 16, 94
    RJ Reynolds Tobacco Co.: pp. 12, 15, 24, 26, 31, 36, 42, 92
    Virginia Slims: pp. 50, 52

South Carolina Department of Health and Environmental
Control: p. 89

Author/Consultant Biographies

Author

Ann Malaspina began her journalism career writing for a community newspaper in Boston. Since 1998, she has been writing nonfiction books for young people. She has written on many topics, including children's rights, American history, and endangered species.

Consultant

Wade Berrettini, the consultant for *Smoking: The Dangerous Addiction*, received his MD from Jefferson Medical College and a PhD in Pharmacology from Thomas Jefferson University. For ten years, Dr. Berrettini served as a Fellow at the National Institutes of Health in Bethesda, Maryland, where he studied the genetics of behavioral disorders. Currently Dr. Berrettini is the Karl E. Rickels Professor of Psychiatry and Director, Center for Neurobiology and Behavior at the University of Pennsylvania in Philadelphia. He is also an attending physician at the Hospital of the University of Pennsylvania.

Dr. Berrettini is the author or co-author of more than 250 scientific articles as well as several books. He has conducted ground-breaking genetic research in nicotine addiction. He is the holder of two patents and the recipient of several awards, including recognition by Best Doctors in America 2003–2004, 2005–2006, and 2007–2008.